To See the Moon

by Hazel Warren

Published in Great Britain in 2019
by Big White Shed, Nottingham
www.bigwhiteshed.co.uk
Printed and bound by Boooksfactory EU

ISBN 978-1-9164035-8-1
Copyright © Hazel Warren 2019
Cover Design by Steve O'Brien 1512design

A CIP catalogue record for this book is available from the British Library.

For all those who wave at crows...

Contents

WINDOW

Spider's Silk

You drew the sunlight from me
spun it
collected it
stored it for weaving.
When the day was done
me – hardly believing
you did not stop
but drew forth
as fine as hair
a silver thread of moonlight
I barely knew was there.

Saturday Matinee

The backdrop is a light blue sky
as brushstroke clouds drift by.

In the foreground a red roof
motionless, catches the sunlight
awaiting its cue to strike up the chorus
whilst mid-stage, a lone fir dances
to communicate the wind
a little too tall
a little too green
a little too much movement.

You can't help but admire his exuberance.

The critics may pan this show
but I, unselfconsciously applaud
the theatre scene through my bedroom window.
Rewarded
in the final act:

The rainbow
an unexpected cameo.

The Moon is Full of Sorrow

The moon is full
I call you to view it:
Have you seen the moon?

We stand together
apart
side-by-side
you had to come to the bathroom to view it

so, side-by-side
in this intimate space, we stand
looking at the moon

and it is beautiful.

You talk of campfires and open space
as I breathe the night air
through the open window
I feel the space around me

the moon is full
and your face is full of sorrow

I want to touch you
to tell you it will be ok
all this will pass
that you're on the right path

I want to remind you
that the most important thing
is to be true
and to breathe
and to see the moon

but instead, I just breathe
and stand by you
looking at the moon

and it is beautiful.

The moon is full
this moment is full
of potential
and it is beautiful.

Flesh and Mortar

Girl and House made a pact:
I will be your home, said House.
Bricks and mortar.

I will share my life with you, said Girl.
Flesh, and blood, and desire, and will.

House knuckled, to have been given such a charge.
Girl smiled, *the bank may own you*
bricks and mortar
but I will make myself belong

bricks and mortar are only so strong
together we will forge a bond beyond
blood and bricks
and flesh and mortar.

In the garden, we'll grow veg
keep chickens
cut flowers for the table
where we will write and paint
and nurture friendships
as we talk deep into the night
spilling red wine on your floor.

Your four walls will be filled with music
and laughter
and sometimes tears will be spilt
and blood as well no doubt
watering these roots we're setting down.

We'll get a cat
and as his claws mark notches on your woodwork
we will feel the seasons turning.

Who knows where it will take us.
Not all journeys are about moving, said Girl
I am learning.

Some journeys only begin when the moving's done,
said House

I always knew this to be true.

Brew Love

Do you want a brew love?

Don't tell me this is true love. Sit beside me, read a book, you wash up, but let me cook.

I hate hoovering. I could get a cleaner. There's something that I like about your demeanour. I'm willing to share if you don't take too much. We can go out for dinner, but we'll always go Dutch.

And you'll have to drip feed me. I can't take all at once. Don't want all encompassing deep feeling, pick me up, take me out, and scrape me off the ceiling.

All I want's a brew love.

In this one part of my life, I'm happy to go slow-mo. Not jump in both feet first, but nurturing the slow-grow. So, let's take our time.

Not race to car crash ending, but learning bit by bit to trust in this befriending, and see where it leads us.

Into rosy sunset, or down the garden path.

Let's enjoy the journey.

Don't think too hard about the destination, I like my solitude, and for your information, to me it doesn't feel like cold isolation, but more like freedom.

Having room to breathe.

Because there's three in this relationship, there's you, me, and the space in between. Each needs an equal share, so don't rush me, don't push me, don't ask me to declare my feelings.

I'm feeling fine and this is good, but I need time.

I do like you, you must know that. But I don't think your mum needs to buy a new hat. Not yet. It's early, and it's just dawning on me that you might be worth getting to know.

So I might let you in.
This is the hallway of my soul, this is where we begin.

I'm holding my breath, for all that's unsaid, and not knowing what's inside your head, all, some, or none of the above.

All I'm asking is do you want a brew love?

Is it Always Night in Space?
Tim Peake straps his sleeping bag loosely to the wall, zips himself in and floats off to sleep.

Drifting off to sleep, so deep
into the cosmos.
Dreams float by amongst shooting stars
and distant moons
amongst black, black, black of
                              – night or day?
                                        Is it always night in space?

This gentle human sleeping
                        drifting,
                                    floating,
                    flying,
                        dreaming.

As a child he dreamt of space
and now, so small and far away.
Drifting
            Floating.
                    Gentle breathing.

                    Rising

                falling.

                No gravity

                            contstrains his dreams.

                        And does he dream

                                of Earth?

16

Mornings Like These

The cold air bites my lungs
as bright grey light
reflects and refracts
the low lying mist
of an old film Noir.

The sun seems lazy
on days like these
barely rising above my knee
barely a drop of blue
breaks through
the white-grey covering
of heavy quilted cloud.

Smother me
muffle all noise
all sharpness gone
blurring boundaries of self.
Sink into my bones
the white-grey fog.
How I love
mornings like these.

Communication Meditation

Communication is the journey
not the destination
there's so much more to be conveyed
than simple information.

Boundaries of identity
are defined through interaction
the most successful of which can lead to
satisfaction.

By contributing and learning
we share an education
knowledge-growth
and thought-creation.

Uncover understanding.
Discover a universe
within our use of words and verse.

Dynamics are negotiated
not finite or fixed
ever changing with ebb and flow
I give you Full Stop.
You hold it
and go.

A delicate dance
along winding boundaries
between what is and what is not
the certain and the impossible
the inappropriate and the unacceptable.

The within and without
and without a doubt
the taken for granted
the unwritten rules
the unstated, understated
the dreams of fools
who danced this way once

but tripped and fell
unwittingly falling under a spell
which was never wittingly cast.

Clumsily grasping for future or past.

But we are in moment
which already passed by
the only way to catch it
was to really not try.

So let your modal verbs go
silence contrition
language is moving
flow with the transition

go with the beat
take a chance
take a bow.

Take a great leap of faith
and begin again

now.

The Day the Rain Came

The sun belted down
for three whole weeks
before that rain came
and quenched our thirst
drenched parched earth
as we laughed, spinning
arms flung wide, grinning
to welcome in
a new beginning

In Spring

You kissed me
and blossoms opened on the trees
declaring to the sky
it is spring!

Midnight Snack

Where is the light that never goes out?
Does the fridge light go out when you shut the door?
How can you know, can you really be sure?

Didn't the Greeks think that light rays come from your eyes?
But what about when you're looking for something in the dark?
Creeping through the night time
Feeling for a light switch…

I find the kitchen
a soft glow.

It is you
looking for something.
Just a little something.

You grin
a girl with a plan.

Soft glow from the fridge
illuminates your skin.

Just a little something.
I'll get the plates.

Train to Sheffield

Dirty windows
dirty sky
wintery trees
rolling by
squares of grass
a shed in each
dirty fields
soggy sheep

Blessing

I won't wish for a sky of blue
or flat seas for your voyage.
I'll wish instead your North is true
and that you have the courage
to ride out any storm together.
When horizons sway and shift
when your ship is hit by treacherous waves
my wish is that they lift
one up to be the moon
to draw the others ebbing tides
forming pebbles, and grains of sand so tiny
to make pearls
for ocean foam and spray so fine
to create weather systems
cumulative forces
working in unison
to shift landscapes
to form glaciers
to feed rivers
to carve new worlds.
What I wish for you
is not flat sea, blue skies above
I wish instead for a sturdy hull
adventure, strength, and love.

You Go Together

You go together like milk and honey
like flip flops and sunny days
sand crunching between your toes
the smell of adventure on the horizon
and nobody knows, which way you'll go next
but you'll go there together
because you go together
like ice-cream and hot weather
or like salt and vinegar
sprinkled on chips
eaten straight from the bag
on the way home.

You go together like coffee
with a Sunday morning
bleary eyed, stretching, still yawning
and just as your day is dawning
your whole life stretches out before you
and you can draw the map.

Never fail to conspire
to inspire one another
to Great Acts.

This is your gift, the truth of this pact.

So think of one another, before any other
and when you're making plans
make your plans together

because together
you are more
than the sum of your parts
when you align your dreams
with one another's hearts.

Alice

I always felt more of an affinity with the rabbit
frantic, rushing, chased or chasing
late for something – no time for wasting
no time to explain, to stupid girl
come on, catch up, you're in *my* world.

But in the end
we had to pity Alice
the image of a lonely girl
tracing raindrops trickling
a tickling of fancies
a prickling the imagination
a literary creation.

And just like life
there is sometimes rhyme
but not necessarily reason:
So why *is* a raven like a writing desk?

INSIDES

You Shouldn't Be Able to Touch Your Insides

My Brother
Destroyer
Destructor
Confider
Protector
Tormentor
Instructor

Lies on that bed, with all tubes going in, looking half dead. On
his lips, a sly grin

My Brother
Teller of Tales
long and short
Entertainer
Proclaimer
Cross
to my Nought

Beckons me over to share his new trick: *Hey Hazel, come 'ere,*
this is pretty sick

That was back before 'sick' meant what it means now
He meant *this is gross:*
Let me just show you how
where the stitches are wide
at the edge of the wound
I can reach right inside with my finger,
there's room!
I can feel my intestines

But Robin!
I feel I must intervene:
You should not be able
to touch your spleen

Have a go he says. *It don't hurt, it's easy*
But internal organs – they make me feel queasy
I faint

My Brother
Scientist
Investigator
Pacifist
Arsonist
Argument Instigator

My Brother
Indestructible
Destroyer of Toys

I fainted.

In truth, I won't lie
I fainted that day

because I thought you might die.

News 24

Does anyone really need twenty–
four hour news feed on twenty–
four seven? As I come and go it's
hard to ignore, in this waiting area
it's more than a bore, being fed
minute–by–minute updates of the latest
scandal or disaster. Not providing
knowledge our intellect to master.
Just feeding fear, from fear, breeds hatred.
With repetition of mere headlines,
questions go undebated. No in–depth
a n a l y s i s, b e c a u s e
sound bites are easier to swallow.

And what of the stories they
choose not to follow? Despite
minute–by–minute tracking of daily
events there are some surprising
omis sions. Might they cause
offence? Not align with the dominant
ideology? Which informs what we are to see?

I find it offensive that without my
consent, they can infiltrate my
day, my eyes, my mind. With a
stream of alarming images, to
which I've become alarmingly blind.

I walk past scenes of horrific human suffering. As words scroll across the screen. I can't help but read about the death of a granny at the hands of a teen.

Yet I don't feel any better informed and I'm not at all prepared. This is not how, or when, or where I would choose to consume news.

I end up feeling violated. Like News 24 is peddling hatred. Can we just turn it off? I don't appreciate it. It's like I'm be ing indoctrinated in some kind of dystopian future.

I'd prefer silent contemplation to these attention grabbing shock tactics designed for desensitisation.

Can we just turn it off?

Not On The Label: What Really Goes into the Food on Your Plate.
Penguin Books (2004) Felicity Lawrence.

"The police don't bother you if you stay in the agricultural area,
but if you stray into town it's another story," he said. "You feel
persecuted on all sides. You have no papers, so you limit your
movements; you fear being stopped and deported, so you hide. You
can take no leisure, you cannot be yourself. You give up all idea of
yourself. Many people break. We survive by supporting each other
and remembering the injustice."

"They had all arrived in boats, having paid the going rate of £1,000
to intermediaries to secure a place with the smugglers. They had
lived in the shack for two and a half years, and three of them had
managed to get official papers. They were legal. Most of them were
in debt after their journey, their families back home providing surety.
They had jobs on the big farm down the road. When there was work
they earned 30 euros a day. If there was enough work they ate,
if there wasn't they didn't. There was no water or sanitation, only
closed irrigation pipes for the crops, so they collected water from a
tank for agricultural effluent. They were often ill with headaches and
stomach trouble.

What if the farmer discovered them here, I asked. Would they be
forced to move on? "But he knows, he comes to pick us up in the
morning in his van," they said. They were getting nervous, so I went
back down towards the road, happy to escape the stench, and
passed the water tank. It was scummy, with three empty pesticide
containers floating in it."

Thirst for Life
for the migrant workers on a Spanish tomato farm

Fresh water
grows tall strong plants
bearing red ripe fruit.

Fresh water
delivered via pipes
that run for miles
as far as eyes can see.

Where eyes can't see,
outside in dust and dirt.
Hidden shadows
in cracked parched earth.

Running, but not free,
live cracked, parched men.

No fresh water
runs for them.

Hostile Environment

Make the environment hostile
spewing vile bile.
Unwelcome.
Until no more come.
Until all have gone.

Playing God

Playing God
the tyrant.

Displacing those
who deign
to set down
roots

in a patch
of Earth
not theirs.

Over there
you are a flower.
Over here,
a weed.

After the Funeral

All property is theft
we used to joke
about the Earl Grey
remember?

Steal what you can
steal a glance
steal a kiss
I steel myself for what's to come

I wish we could have stolen more time
before the grandest theft of all
the greatest heist
that stole you away

I'll put the kettle on
for the fourteenth time today
boil up another cliché

time heals all
tea and time
the great healers.

Proper tea ain't theft.
Mortali-ty.
That's the one to watch for.

Renovation

Sun shines down
on a small cottage
birds squabble over blackberries.
She is digging
undercover
undermining the foundations.
Following Tommy-knockers
to ever deepening veins
blind and uncertain
she cannot see to place her feet.

Surfacing for air
she is surprised to find daylight
and you, waiting
in the kitchen.

The afternoon sun casts
a gentle glow.
The shadow
of an overgrown blackberry bush
falls across your arm.

As you talk
the wallpaper picking begins
the way the corners curl disturbs her.
Next, she is chipping away plaster
and breathing cool fresh air
you notice the window
has been smashed.

You agree to sleep on it
but she wakes, to find
you have removed the roof
leaving only cool air on her skin
and the taste of blackberries
in her mouth.

Lost

Deep in this forest
you planted seeds of hope.
In dappled sunlight they sprouted
took root in warm soil.

In spring
dared to stretch out
grateful green shoots.

Now it is summer
delicate flowers
not yet fully formed.

You unwittingly threaten
to rip them out.

Should I chain myself?
Protest?
To whom can I appeal?
Is this some abhorrent test?

I had believed you when you said it
I think you believed it too
but now we are discovering
that perhaps, it isn't true.

Mother's Day

Silently
child glues yellow crepe paper
to pink card.

A crappy card
she makes for no one.

Eyes down to avoid their stares

*If I can't see you
I am invisible
I am indivisible
You cannot break me
I am the lowest prime*

Later the missing mother's mother
will find the card and weep.

A silent tear
shared with no one.

Eyes averted
if we never speak

Can we pretend it isn't happening?

Emotions reigned back in
the card goes in the bin.

We move on
separately.
Guardians of each other's solitary silence.

That Room
(in response to Andrea Gibson's poem "Tell Me…")

I cannot tell you about that room
or why fresh paint smells of despair
and comfort is a well-worn coat
or unchanged sheets
or a re-found, long-lost bear
balding, with a button for a nose
I could give you my childhood in a box
and still you would not know.

Desolation

Seeing you
is like picking a scab.
Irresistible
but tinged
with a morbid fascination
like revisiting the site
of some old devastation.
You are Pompeii.
You are Chernobyl.
I should stay away
but don't know if I'm able.
I'm placing a bet
that I'm bound to lose
because, seeing you
is like pressing a bruise.
I only do it
to check that it still hurts.

The Dancer Dies Twice

Hours of servitude
      raised up on tippy toe
            for the longest time

        Hold it.
        Hold it.
        Hold it.
           Breathe!

                She was magnificent
           life itself
       breathed into the music
let it flow, lifted up
       spiralling dizzy heights.

Take in the view and smile, they are all here for you.

The noise
when bone and cartilage crunched
she felt nothing.

     Ethereal
       Still floating above
             this toned body
                this gracious vessel
           the lower limb, twisted
       unreal, misshapen
   mistaken?

       But no.
       Onwards to consultant
       and surgeon and physio.

The day they told her the news
she crumbled
collapsed and buckled
cried out a deathly wail

Hold it.
Hold it.
Hold it.
Breathe!

Shaking
Shoulders heaving
for the longest time.
For a life time.
She'd danced her last dance
And died.

This first death
the hardest to bear.

In response to *A Dancer Dies Twice*. Produced by Eleanor McDowall,
a Falling Tree production for BBC Radio 4. A documentary about first
deaths and last dances, and what happens when an instrument as
finely tuned as a dancer's body begins to change

*"A dancer dies twice, once when they stop dancing,
and this first death is the most painful"*.
Martha Graham, Choreographer

Sea Air: on missing a friend

My eyes stop on your number
Why is it still in my phone?
I don't delete it,
I keep it.

A memento
A pretence
A lie

I could always phone - you pretend you're out
let's pretend you didn't die.

I came across a photograph
it caught me unaware
it's back before the chemo took your hair

You're looking well
must be before we knew
what ached and grew inside of you.

When I close my eyes
bring you to mind,
it is the you of that holiday by the sea.

You couldn't walk
we talked and talked
laughed about how you used to be worried
over incidental things.

Faced with monumental struggle
you felt calm and able.
When body weakened
you found inner strength to fight.

My turn to worry.
I fretted as you winced
you ached, but did not complain
said you liked the sea air on your face
didn't even mind the rain

said you were tired

said you weren't done yet

I doubted
but you defied expectations and fought
more than I thought possible.
You survived so much
so many times

and just when I started to believe
you really were invincible
you proved me wrong a second time.

You never said goodbye.

I miss you
I'm sad that it took all that
to reveal to you, your strength
to let you know your character.

I hope you believed it in the end.

I still miss my friend.

I'm sorry we didn't get to see more
of that feisty, determined soul
that it had to burn you up to let you know.

Is there poetry in this learning to love,
to know yourself
no self-doubt left
leave life behind
and slip into death.

Maybe not
Maybe you'd have said
there's no poetry in dying
and went still screaming
"I'm not done yet."

I'll still think of you
sea air in your face.

As for me?
I just miss my friend.

Black Lace Weaver Spider
note the life cycle of the female Black Lace Weaver Spider

Black, for the darkest depths of my soul
my love for you unending.

Black for the night, I lay in wait
for you to consume me whole.

Intricate lace, this web I am weaving
funeral lace, black with delicate breathing.

I have woven my history
our tapestry and
tap
      tap
            tap

I draw you to me

without a little trepidation, this gentle vibration
awakens sensation
amongst a spidery congregation

an army marches

my Spidery Children
my Black Lace Weavers

at long last, you break your fast
the first course, I laid for you

vibrations, as I tremble
I draw you on to feast.

Feed well, and mother will serve.

Farewell.

One evening, my daughter
heavy with eggs

will revisit instinctual memory
consult the family tapestry
to find - matricide

and as is natural
filled with birth, she will gaze at death

don her mother's funeral lace
threaded throughout and woven within.

Just as sure as history repeat

well, just as sure
the children must eat.

Black, for the darkest depths of her soul.
Her love for them unending.

Black for the night she lies in wait
for them to consume her whole.

No Physical Trace

No lipstick mark, upon a cup.
No strand of hair, within the brush.
There was no physical trace, that you were ever here
but sometimes, a glitch in the matrix appears.
Blue biro, scrawled within a book
which I can only hold and look.
These secret communications are a little one-sided.
I wrote you a letter, my feelings confided
but you will never gaze upon my pen mark.

It is only later, much later
that I am to learn
that you were in everything
seen at every turn
an algorithm, for those that held the key.
They remember you planting that tree.

Loved those orange curtains
the choice of tableware
for them, the presence of a piano
proof enough, that you were always there.
For me? It still seemed a little one-sided
and more than a little unfair
because I lived in the distance you left in his stare
grew up wishing, that I wasn't there.
From a hospital bed, where he could not meet my eye
to a psychiatrist's office, where we both refused to cry.
We are not so different, my Dad and I.

We both miss you
so I guess we're similar that way too
but somehow the subject became a taboo
and it seemed so one-sided
it felt so unfair
that you were a secret
that he couldn't share.

(It turns out, you can miss something you never had
-I just wish someone would've told my Dad.)

Darkness and Light

How does the darkness make you feel?

Safe

Safe?

Hidden away
Secret
Closed in
Snug and safe
in the darkness

It's not only you can hide in the darkness
How does the light make you feel?

Cold

Cold?

Open
Exposed
Naked and cold

Bring my coverlet of darkness
turn the lights down low
bring my eiderdown
black as coal

Shut out the sun
with a black cloud shroud
mask my face from your radiance
I must be alone

The darkness and solitude
they feel like

Home

GROWING

Grass

The grass is greener over there
see how lush it grows.

It would grow here too
if you would only water it
nurture it, tend to it and
rake the leaves, but

lawns take time to establish.

Trouble is,
I'm not sure I want
a manicured lawn
with shed in the corner for your tools.

I want a meadow
growing wild and free
tiny, yellow, flowers
floating thigh high.

I look back to find desire lines
have cut through the meadow
grass trampled, the mud shows

I see your lawn
the grass is greener over there
see how lush it grows.

Cycling Proficiency

A lady named Sheila
rode her bike to the shop
meanwhile in France
the Tour, was rocked
she is making a mockery
an amateur, barely proficient
got all the gear, but no idea
her amateur outing, would make cyclists fear
their credibility damaged.

Victoria Pendleton took great offence
these shoddy cyclists should drop the pretence
cycling proficiency isn't enough
we need to sort the wheat from the chuff!

How the hell are we meant to know who's for real
when anyone riding around on two wheels
can say they're a cyclist, on their own report.
It's making a farce of our beautiful sport.

They need to be stopped
to be stamped on, and shamed
their ridiculous bells
their whistles and chains.

Don't they know, that I studied
hard and long.
So anyone who doesn't
do it my way
is wrong!

To Do List

Wash Up
Clean House
Sort life
Phone Dad
Smile for no reason
Run for no reason
Commit small act of treason
Question your beliefs
Believe your answers
Listen
Listen to your heart
Fall in love
Fall in the sea
Fall to your knees
Scream
Louder
Stop.
Repeat points 4, 6, 9 and 10
Write a letter
Right a wrong
Tell a tale
Sing a song
Scream your lyrics
into a hole in a tree
Whistle your own melody
Believe that you can be free
Dance stepping sideways and back
Come off the rails
Get back on track
Scream again
this time into the sea
Feel grateful
For the waves who wash your soul
with wish, wash, wish, wash
in, out
never ending
Inhale
Constant, ever changing
Exhale

Take a pen

Write a list

This time be sure
to do all the things you missed

Evidence of Life

The milk has turned to cheese
the bin is flowing over
teabags in the sink
15 centimetres from the compost tub
why would you do that?

A bag half unpacked
a picture frame cracked
in the midst of this chaos
a nest.

Evidence of habitation
blanket creates a comfort wall
a glass
a saucer
crumbs
a book.

You were here
your comfortable oasis
oblivious to surrounding debris.

Home

Green and yellow patchwork
against slate blue hues of sky
grinning like idiots
the miles, stretching our smiles
which in turn stretch our vowels.*

I expected some bitterness
return of some old hurt on this trip
but instead I'm filled with wonder
at how far we've come
and what we had to leave behind
were we so blind?

I breathe the landscape in
as we carry the sun up the hill
sharing its weight between us
and the river glistens
off cold grey walls
and trees are reflected
on the reflections of trees.

I recognise the recognition
creeping across your face.
Home is a feeling
but once, it was a place.

*ow – err, vow-ells

Goal Posts

I'm thinking of football
jumpers for goal posts and gender roles
and who's most hard done by
generation's expectations, all to play for
and how it's ok for a girl to be 'boyish'
the tomboy -so strong
but for a boy to be 'girlish'?
well, that's just wrong.

He shall not wear pink, or play with dolls
and tea sets are forbidden!

All this really reflects is the utter contempt
in which society holds: The Female
these trinkets, that symbolise 'girl'
to be 'girlish', to be soft or caring?
to be small, meek, weak
to never be daring
or brave, or bold

to be humble and small
and show your strength
only in a quiet way
that lets your brother stand tall.

The Ballad of Laura Bassett

She was in it, to win it
but own-goaled the last minute
dreams were dashed there
hopes were trashed
I don't care for football but
Laura Bassett
your tragedy
touched me.

Dig for Victory

First I dug my heels in, childishly refusing to move on
from the site of childhood trauma.
Later I dug my nails in, until my palms bled red
next I dug deep within, I searched my soul
and found it, wanting
lacking.

Searched in others, to find them
wanting
lacking
empty souls waiting to be fed.

Now, I dig in soil
plant seeds of hope
and bleed from thorny brambles
which I wrestle for the fruit
red juice stains my palms.

Watering

Listening to the sun set
under birdsong and in still air
tranquil watering
inspecting leaf and stalk
searching soil
where gentle sprouts of green
interrupt the brown

Weeding

With the skill of a surgeon
gloved hand steady
firm grasp
gently easing to and fro
to loosen first
before
with slow satisfaction
the threaded root
is pulled
like a varicose vein

Return of the Senses

I woke one morning and the
whole world glowed with autumn.
Petrichor filled up my senses
my nostrils alive.

Crunching leaves sang out my every step
I slowed to enjoy the song
my very soul endures.

These moments
of not sensing endurance
but sensing alive
tasting the air
as wind brings life to trees.

I felt my body dissolve.
These atoms, nothing new.
What is knowledge?
Energy is never lost
only transferred.
I remember the day I learned
about atoms.
Can I breathe you in?

This universe
to which we all belong
we cannot make claim, or own
or scream is wrong.

All this knowledge and experience
all the things we accrue

it's just atoms
breaking apart
and joining anew.

This Place is Ours

We wandered the streets
pointing out our childhood
every detail that remains
a teenaged memory
clambering rooftops of shops
shady trees by the river
we knew each and every one
every hiding place and secret spot.

The record shop has gone.
They cleaned the statues
and dared to move them round.
The library?
Now a shiny glass box
up the top of town
no longer by the river
where we sat and read
reminding me of something
Siddhartha might have said.

This place is ours
it shaped us
we abandoned it
escaped.
This place nurtured
and we moved on
and now, although it makes no sense
I can't help feeling hurt
that the record shop has gone.

20 Years

Are we flirting? I want to ask because I'm not sure, but I know that asking is against the rules, and I'm not sure what the rules are but I'm pretty sure that's one, because it's got to be done subtly. Cloak and dagger. Hide and seek. I'm wearing my best underwear but you won't know because I didn't want to seem too keen. So black lace and tiny straps remain hidden under baggy shirt and jeans.

Are we flirting? I need to know, I'm choking. I get globus when I feel strong emotion and I think I saw you look at me. You held your gaze too long. Don't give the game away. We're doing this all wrong. I'm not good at this, but you know me all too well. You were my first love twenty years ago. Should be long enough, but I'm back on that bridge watching shooting stars, tucked inside your leather jacket like a sparrow, and it was easy then, because I knew that I was yours, but now I'm scared because it seems so easy with you now.

Are we flirting? I have to know because you're texting me goodnight, and you still make me laugh. I felt like I hadn't laughed like that since you last made me laugh. I feel like I've been waiting to see you, well, since I saw you last, and I'm flickering in between feeling so at ease and my heart being in my mouth when I think of what it means.

Are we flirting? I have to know because I'm scared, and you're the only one that can make me feel self-assured. So are we? Flirting? If I ask it will be ruined, so I'm skirting round the edges, like some kind of clumsy moth, trying to avoid landing on the spot. Trying not to get burnt by that flickering flame, which provides some light, but not enough to focus on the -What?

Are we flirting? I've got to know because I can't see how this is going to end, and I don't know if you're a lover or a friend and if this feels so familiar just because it's old, or because it's you and me.

And I thought that story had been told.

Beyond Fireworks and Glitter Balls

This love is music
it is a dawn chorus
more ancient than a brontosaurus.

This love has been waiting for you
it is in stardust
in tectonic shifts of Earth's crust
and the comfort of your hair, brushed
in the knowledge that you can trust
this love *will* share its dinner with you.

It is excitement of butterflies in your tummy
a steadying hand when you're feeling funny
so when your dreams seem distant, out of reach
let this love lift you both up
cloud layer; breached
to find that when you're together
blue skies prevail whatever the weather.

From the grandest gesture to the gentlest whisper
two souls head deep into the night.
Dance beyond the fireworks and glitter balls
through trees and fairy lights.

Let this love be the laughter that makes your cheeks ache
and from dusk into daybreak
this love will hold you
'till sunrise turns your
whole
sky
golden.

Symbiotic Semantics

A large mammal
warms its skin
under Serengeti skies
the perfect breeding ground
for multitude of tics and various flying insects
which bite and suck
the sweet tasting blood.

A small bird lands
resting lightly on the breadth of this back
sating its hunger
relieving the mammal
of its parasitic irritants.

Some might say "co-dependent"
but I prefer symbiotic.

Stealing Fire From Heaven

Sharing secrets in the darkness
we reel off a list of guilt and shame
all the lies, mistakes and pain
emptying our own Pandora's box
we find that in the bottom there remains

Hope.

We hold it carefully in our hands
equal parts confidence and desire
a gentle resection and dissection occurs.

Our hopes aligned.

Giggling
at the enormity
of our honesty
we peeled back layers
of vulnerability

and beneath all this
it is Love we find.

Roots to Branches

Love is the answer
when the questions howl
brace together
against any storm that blows.
These arms are the arms
that will hold you.
Hold steady.
These feet are planted by yours
your roots entangling.
These hands will hold yours
so hold steady.
For these eyes will see you
a vision, even in the darkest night
and come morning
dawn will break
and see you are not broken
but risen like the sun
and whole, together
branches waving
reaching skyward
as dappled light plays
on dancing leaves.

THE END

Acknowledgments

I wrote a book. I can hardly believe you are holding this object in your hands. Without Frank McMahon and DIY poets this book would simply not exist, thank you for introducing me to the poetry scene, providing support and encouragement to write, friendly feedback and criticism on early works and for opportunities to read, listen, perform and grow. The Nottingham poetry scene is full of creatives who continue to inspire and encourage, thank you to all the facilitators who keep the scene alive, create safe spaces and understand the need for bad poems, for unpolished performances, for mistakes. You create a community in which to share. I see you.

Thanks to everyone who repeatedly asked when I was going to do a book, here it is. This is for you. Some people believed in the project enough to pre-order, helping with production costs before production. Special thanks to John Humphreys for his comments on the initial read through of a first draft of collected poems, and for telling me to do it. Sorry I didn't include Tracy for you.

Leanne Moden has helped me in more ways than she can know, she kindly gave her time to talk about how to translate the words in my head to the paper and pointed me towards Anne Holloway at Big White Shed, who agreed to meet, chat, believed in the project from the outset, and provided generous and invaluable advice and support. I really enjoyed working with Anne on editing and for advice on every aspect of putting a book together. I've learnt a lot.

One day over lunch and a walk I talked to Steve O'Brien about a vague idea for book design, he responded enthusiastically, listened to my ideas and went on to create several options for the cover, some of which included my initial thoughts, I think what you made was much better. Thanks for humouring me and for creating this design, better than anything I could have imagined.

There are a few poems in this book which have been read at very special occasions, thanks to Belinda and Gaz, Julia and Will, Ruth and Tim and Maureen and Peter for letting me share words written for you. Massive love to you all. With eyes for accuracy, Maureen McNamara and Peter Tobin kindly agreed to proof read the final copy, so any mistakes – please report to them.

Thanks to everyone and anyone who unwittingly provided the content of any of these poems. I hope you don't mind me sharing them. Thanks especially to my family for letting me share some very personal interpretations of events which affected us all. Finally thanks to JC and P, who listen, encourage, keep me (reasonably) sane, and provide distractions and perspective when it all gets a bit much. I love you.

Hazel Warren is a member of the DIY poets and Paper Cranes collectives. She is an organiser of the International Women's Day event *Women Say... Stuff*. She has performed in cafes and pubs, bottle shops and book shops, at festivals including Gateway to Southwell, Green Man, Splendour, Indie Beer Feast, Nottingham Night Light, Nottingham Poetry Festival and will be appearing at Edinburgh Free Fringe 2019.

To See the Moon is Hazel's debut collection. She has been published previously in the *Best of DIY* collections and online by Burning House Press www.burninghousepress.com (where some of these poems have previously appeared). She also contributed artwork to *Woman* published by Mud Press (2016). You can find Hazel performing at open mic nights and DIY events around Nottingham, the East Midlands and occasionally further afield. She sometimes wields a ukulele for musical forays and a pencil for artistic endeavours, and responds well to praise. Follow her on twitter or Instagram @hazeleypoos